EXCEPTIONALLY HUMAN®
COMMUNICATION WORKBOOK

Brian Shapiro

Shapiro Communications Publishing
2019

First Printing 2019

ISBN: 978-0-9972848-3-6

Shapiro Communications Publishing
245 S. 16th Street
Philadelphia, PA 19102

www.shapirocommunications.com

You are already a good communicator. You naturally communicate well with the partners, co-workers, customers, family, and friends in your life. You would not have been able to develop the relationships you have with them if that were not the case. So the goal is not to become a good communicator, but rather to become an *Exceptionally Human* communicator. *Exceptionally Human* communicators are strategic, nimble, and can connect to a variety of people in a variety of settings. To that end, acquiring new communication skills is the goal and establishing a clear pathway towards that goal is key.

The Johari Window Model

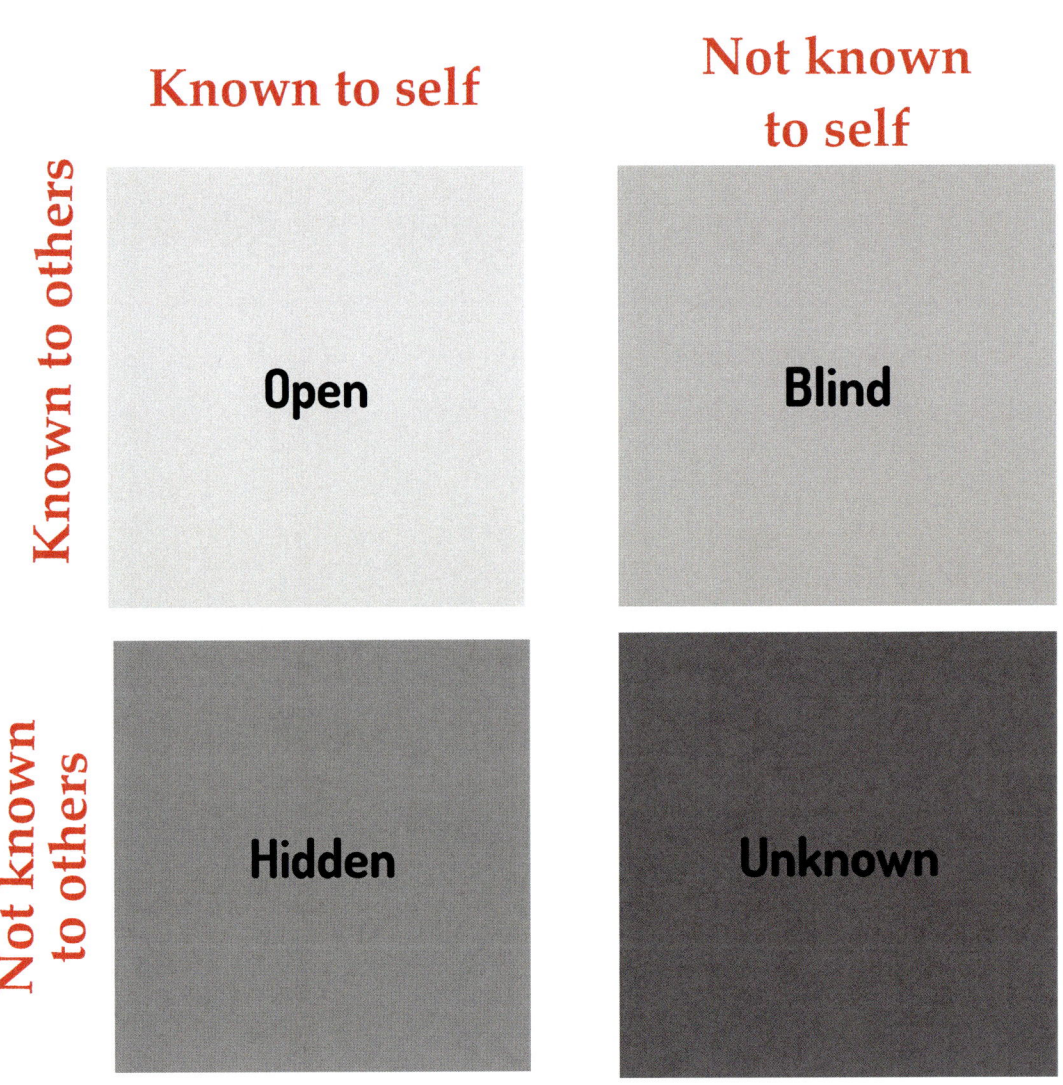

	Known to self	Not known to self
Known to others	Open	Blind
Not known to others	Hidden	Unknown

How do you communicate?

OPEN : Qualities about how you communicate that you know about yourself
AND other people know about you as well.

_____

_____

_____

_____

_____

HIDDEN: Qualities about how you communicate that you know about
yourself BUT other people don't know about you.

_____

_____

_____

_____

_____

BLIND: Qualities about how you communicate that you didn't know
about yourself UNTIL someone else pointed it out to you.

_____

_____

_____

_____

_____

THE THREE PILLARS OF EXCEPTIONAL COMMUNICATION

If you take the time to consider those people who have communicated the most effectively with you, a few things should come to mind:

- First, they are typically people you perceive as **credible, or people you trust**.
- Second, they are probably people, who when you think of them, **elicit more positive emotions than negative ones**. In other words, you generally feel good when they come to mind.
- Finally, when they are communicating with you, you'll more often than not perceive their communication to be **clear, reasonable, and rational**.

TRUST

Trust refers to your credibility, or how much trust you earn from others. You are only as trustworthy as other people perceive you to be. Trust in you will elevate or diminish based on how you communicate; with the (actions) always outweighing the words.

Ask yourself - Am I using the right tone, speech rate, word choice, and communication method to demonstrate to others that I am trustworthy?

EMOTIONS

Emotions refers to the emotional response, or feelings generated in the person you are communicating with. Understand the other person's feelings, and how your communication style is impacting them.

Ask yourself - Am I putting myself in the others' place – using empathy – and taking into consideration their emotional state even if it's different from mine?

REASON

Reason refers to how reasonable, rational, and logical the other person finds your position, request or argument to be as they see it.

Ask yourself - Does this seem reasonable to them? Is the information clear, accurate and relevant to them?

"Trust is the remarkable force that pulls you over that gap between certainty and uncertainty."
- Rachel Bostman

"...confidence that [one] will find what is desired [from another] rather than what is feared."
– Morton Deutsch

What about a person's communication allows you to experience them as trustworthy?

_____

_____

_____

_____

_____

_____

_____

What about your communication allows other people to experience you as trustworthy?

_____

_____

_____

_____

_____

_____

EMOTIONS   What emotions are being elicited?

"There is nothing either good or bad, but thinking makes it so."
– William Shakespeare's **Hamlet**

"I've learned that people will forget what you said, people will forget what you did, but people will never forget how you made them feel."
-Maya Angelou

What about a person's communication style influences your emotions, for better or for worse?

_____

_____

_____

_____

_____

_____

What about your communication style influences other people's emotions, for better or worse?

_____

_____

_____

_____

_____

_____

"No matter how reasonable and rational we might find our communication, if what we convey is seen as unreasonable, we begin to erode the very credibility we worked to establish and begin to generate emotions that will cause the other person to be less inclined to listen to us."

\- Brian Shapiro

What about a person's communication allows you to experience them as reasonable?

_____

_____

_____

_____

_____

_____

What about your communication allows other people to experience you as reasonable?

_____

_____

_____

_____

_____

_____

_____

The Shapiro 21 Day Approach

ESTABLISHING A DAILY COMMUNICATION PRACTICE

In order to firmly root any new communication skill, you need to repeat this new skill over and over until it becomes habitual and reflexive. There is no mastery to attain here, rather the continual movement towards mastery that is the goal. In other words, put your energy into a simple, repetitive, daily practice. What's most important is establishing a conscious practice so new communication skills are built up over time.

THE RELATIONSHIP

FIRST, for the next 21 business days, identify ONE specific interaction per day you have with a specific individual. Over these 21 days, you can identify several different individuals or remain focused on just one; it's entirely up to you.

SECOND, identify the current relationship with that person. Is this a superior/subordinate relationship, a collegial relationship, a service provider/client relationship, or something else?

THIRD, identify the status differential between the two of you. Status refers to the power difference between you and the other person. For example, if you are speaking to a superior, organizationally they have higher status than you do, therefore the power difference in this interaction would be your low status to their high status. Of course, the opposite is true if you are speaking to a subordinate, your status is high and theirs is low. If you are speaking to a colleague, your status would be equal.

* It is important to note, that there is also perceived status, or "informal" status. This refers to the status someone believes they have, as opposed to what they formally have. For example, you may have a colleague that, although your "formal" status is equal, they believe they have higher status and like to be communicated with in that way.

FOURTH, identify the interactional goal or desired outcome from this exchange. Try to be as specific as possible.

THE THREE PILLARS IN ACTION

 **TRUST:** The next step is to determine what this person needs from you, communication wise, to perceive you as **TRUSTWORTHY.** You will then determine what you need to do more or less of, communication wise, so you can meet their **TRUST** need. This is when you can refer back to your Johari Window findings for help.

 **EMOTIONS:** Determine what this person needs from you, communication wise, to experience positive **EMOTIONS.** You will then determine what you need to do more or less of, communication wise, so you can meet their **EMOTIONS** need. Again, you can refer back to your Johari Window findings.

 **REASON:** Determine what this person needs from you, communication wise, to perceive you as **REASONABLE.** You will then determine what you need to do more or less of, communication wise, so you can meet their **REASON** needs. Johari again.

 **PERSONAL FEEDBACK:** After the exchange, note down 1) what appeared to work, 2) what didn't work, and 3) what the experience felt like for you (for example, was it awkward, easy, torturous, comfortable, uncomfortable, successful, unsuccessful, etc, and why).

EMBRACING DISCOMFORT

At times, the Shapiro 21 Day Approach will generate discomfort, as often times the unfamiliar brings about such feelings. There's no avoiding this discomfort. The only thing that eases the discomfort is continually practicing this new skill over time. So, as opposed to viewing these uncomfortable feelings as signs that you are doing something wrong, work to embrace the discomfort as a sign you are learning and growing. Embrace the discomfort, transform it into motivation, and savor the reward of learning a new communication skill!

WORKSHEET - Day 1

NAME OF PERSON _____ RELATIONSHIP_____

STATUS DIFFERENCE   (Circle one)   High to Low   Low to High   Equal

Interactional goal? _____

What might they need from me so they experience TRUST?

_____

_____

What might I need to do more/less of?

_____

_____

What might they need from me so they experience POSITIVE EMOTIONS?

_____

_____

What might I need to do more/less of?

_____

_____

What might they need from me to view me as REASONABLE/RATIONAL?

_____

_____

What might I need to do more/less of?

_____

_____

Personal feedback

_____

_____

WORKSHEET - Day 2

NAME OF PERSON _____ RELATIONSHIP_____

STATUS DIFFERENCE   (Circle one)   High to Low   Low to High   Equal

Interactional goal? _____

What might they need from me so they experience TRUST?

_____

_____

What might I need to do more/less of?

_____

_____

What might they need from me so they experience POSITIVE EMOTIONS?

_____

_____

What might I need to do more/less of?

_____

_____

What might they need from me to view me as REASONABLE/RATIONAL?

_____

_____

What might I need to do more/less of?

_____

_____

Personal feedback

_____

_____

WORKSHEET – Day 3

NAME OF PERSON _____ RELATIONSHIP_____

STATUS DIFFERENCE   (Circle one)   High to Low   Low to High   Equal

Interactional goal? _____

What might they need from me so they experience TRUST?

_____

_____

What might I need to do more/less of?

_____

_____

What might they need from me so they experience POSITIVE EMOTIONS?

_____

_____

What might I need to do more/less of?

_____

_____

What might they need from me to view me as REASONABLE/RATIONAL?

_____

_____

What might I need to do more/less of?

_____

_____

Personal feedback

_____

_____

WORKSHEET – Day 4

NAME OF PERSON _____ RELATIONSHIP_____

STATUS DIFFERENCE   (Circle one)   High to Low   Low to High   Equal

Interactional goal? _____

What might they need from me so they experience TRUST?

_____

_____

What might I need to do more/less of?

_____

_____

What might they need from me so they experience POSITIVE EMOTIONS?

_____

_____

What might I need to do more/less of?

_____

_____

What might they need from me to view me as REASONABLE/RATIONAL?

_____

_____

What might I need to do more/less of?

_____

_____

Personal feedback

_____

_____

WORKSHEET – Day 5

NAME OF PERSON _____ RELATIONSHIP_____

STATUS DIFFERENCE   (Circle one)   High to Low   Low to High   Equal

Interactional goal? _____

What might they need from me so they experience TRUST?

_____

_____

What might I need to do more/less of?

_____

_____

What might they need from me so they experience POSITIVE EMOTIONS?

_____

_____

What might I need to do more/less of?

_____

_____

What might they need from me to view me as REASONABLE/RATIONAL?

_____

_____

What might I need to do more/less of?

_____

_____

Personal feedback

_____

_____

WORKSHEET – Day 6

NAME OF PERSON _____ RELATIONSHIP_____

STATUS DIFFERENCE   (Circle one)   High to Low   Low to High   Equal

Interactional goal? _____

What might they need from me so they experience TRUST?

_____

_____

What might I need to do more/less of?

_____

_____

What might they need from me so they experience POSITIVE EMOTIONS?

_____

_____

What might I need to do more/less of?

_____

_____

What might they need from me to view me as REASONABLE/RATIONAL?

_____

_____

What might I need to do more/less of?

_____

_____

Personal feedback

_____

_____

WORKSHEET – Day 7

NAME OF PERSON _____ RELATIONSHIP_____

STATUS DIFFERENCE   (Circle one)   High to Low   Low to High   Equal

Interactional goal? _____

What might they need from me so they experience TRUST?

_____

_____

What might I need to do more/less of?

_____

_____

What might they need from me so they experience POSITIVE EMOTIONS?

_____

_____

What might I need to do more/less of?

_____

_____

What might they need from me to view me as REASONABLE/RATIONAL?

_____

_____

What might I need to do more/less of?

_____

_____

Personal feedback

_____

_____

CONCLUSIONS for Days 1-7

Based upon your Shapiro 21 Day Approach findings, please answer the following:

1. What are 3 communication practices you can do *more* of?

_____

_____

_____

2. What reminders, tools or support would best allow you to do so?

_____

_____

_____

3. What are 3 communication practices you can do *less* of?

_____

_____

_____

4. What reminders, tools, or support would best allow you to do so?

_____

_____

_____

WORKSHEET – Day 8

NAME OF PERSON _____ RELATIONSHIP_____

STATUS DIFFERENCE   (Circle one)   High to Low   Low to High   Equal

Interactional goal? _____

What might they need from me so they experience TRUST?

_____

_____

What might I need to do more/less of?

_____

_____

What might they need from me so they experience POSITIVE EMOTIONS?

_____

_____

What might I need to do more/less of?

_____

_____

What might they need from me to view me as REASONABLE/RATIONAL?

_____

_____

What might I need to do more/less of?

_____

_____

Personal feedback

_____

_____

WORKSHEET - Day 9

NAME OF PERSON _____ RELATIONSHIP_____

STATUS DIFFERENCE   (Circle one)   High to Low   Low to High   Equal

Interactional goal? _____

What might they need from me so they experience TRUST?

_____

_____

What might I need to do more/less of?

_____

_____

What might they need from me so they experience POSITIVE EMOTIONS?

_____

_____

What might I need to do more/less of?

_____

_____

What might they need from me to view me as REASONABLE/RATIONAL?

_____

_____

What might I need to do more/less of?

_____

_____

Personal feedback

_____

_____

WORKSHEET – Day 10

NAME OF PERSON _____ RELATIONSHIP_____

STATUS DIFFERENCE   (Circle one)   High to Low   Low to High   Equal

Interactional goal? _____

What might they need from me so they experience TRUST?

_____

_____

What might I need to do more/less of?

_____

_____

What might they need from me so they experience POSITIVE EMOTIONS?

_____

_____

What might I need to do more/less of?

_____

_____

What might they need from me to view me as REASONABLE/RATIONAL?

_____

_____

What might I need to do more/less of?

_____

_____

Personal feedback

_____

_____

WORKSHEET - Day 11

NAME OF PERSON _____ RELATIONSHIP_____

STATUS DIFFERENCE   (Circle one)   High to Low   Low to High   Equal

Interactional goal? _____

What might they need from me so they experience TRUST?

_____

_____

What might I need to do more/less of?

_____

_____

What might they need from me so they experience POSITIVE EMOTIONS?

_____

_____

What might I need to do more/less of?

_____

_____

What might they need from me to view me as REASONABLE/RATIONAL?

_____

_____

What might I need to do more/less of?

_____

_____

Personal feedback

_____

_____

WORKSHEET – Day 12

NAME OF PERSON _____ RELATIONSHIP_____

STATUS DIFFERENCE   (Circle one)   High to Low   Low to High   Equal

Interactional goal? _____

What might they need from me so they experience TRUST?

_____

_____

What might I need to do more/less of?

_____

_____

What might they need from me so they experience POSITIVE EMOTIONS?

_____

_____

What might I need to do more/less of?

_____

_____

What might they need from me to view me as REASONABLE/RATIONAL?

_____

_____

What might I need to do more/less of?

_____

_____

Personal feedback

_____

_____

WORKSHEET - Day 13

NAME OF PERSON _____ RELATIONSHIP_____

STATUS DIFFERENCE   (Circle one)   High to Low   Low to High   Equal

Interactional goal? _____

What might they need from me so they experience TRUST?

_____

_____

What might I need to do more/less of?

_____

_____

What might they need from me so they experience POSITIVE EMOTIONS?

_____

_____

What might I need to do more/less of?

_____

_____

What might they need from me to view me as REASONABLE/RATIONAL?

_____

_____

What might I need to do more/less of?

_____

_____

Personal feedback

_____

_____

WORKSHEET - Day 14

NAME OF PERSON _____ RELATIONSHIP_____

STATUS DIFFERENCE   (Circle one)   High to Low   Low to High   Equal

Interactional goal? _____

What might they need from me so they experience TRUST?

_____

_____

What might I need to do more/less of?

_____

_____

What might they need from me so they experience POSITIVE EMOTIONS?

_____

_____

What might I need to do more/less of?

_____

_____

What might they need from me to view me as REASONABLE/RATIONAL?

_____

_____

What might I need to do more/less of?

_____

_____

Personal feedback

_____

_____

24

CONCLUSIONS for Days 8-14

Based upon your Shapiro 21 Day Approach findings, please answer the following:

1. What are 3 communication practices you can do *more* of?

_____

_____

_____

2. What reminders, tools or support would best allow you to do so?

_____

_____

_____

3. What are 3 communication practices you can do *less* of?

_____

_____

_____

4. What reminders, tools or support would best allow you to do so?

_____

_____

_____

WORKSHEET – Day 15

NAME OF PERSON _____ RELATIONSHIP_____

STATUS DIFFERENCE   (Circle one)   High to Low   Low to High   Equal

Interactional goal? _____

What might they need from me so they experience TRUST?

_____

_____

What might I need to do more/less of?

_____

_____

What might they need from me so they experience POSITIVE EMOTIONS?

_____

_____

What might I need to do more/less of?

_____

_____

What might they need from me to view me as REASONABLE/RATIONAL?

_____

_____

What might I need to do more/less of?

_____

_____

Personal feedback

_____

_____

WORKSHEET – Day 16

NAME OF PERSON _____ RELATIONSHIP_____

STATUS DIFFERENCE   (Circle one)   High to Low   Low to High   Equal

Interactional goal? _____

What might they need from me so they experience TRUST?

_____

_____

What might I need to do more/less of?

_____

_____

What might they need from me so they experience POSITIVE EMOTIONS?

_____

_____

What might I need to do more/less of?

_____

_____

What might they need from me to view me as REASONABLE/RATIONAL?

_____

_____

What might I need to do more/less of?

_____

_____

Personal feedback

_____

_____

WORKSHEET – Day 17

NAME OF PERSON _____ RELATIONSHIP_____

STATUS DIFFERENCE   (Circle one)   High to Low   Low to High   Equal

Interactional goal? _____

What might they need from me so they experience TRUST?

_____

_____

What might I need to do more/less of?

_____

_____

What might they need from me so they experience POSITIVE EMOTIONS?

_____

_____

What might I need to do more/less of?

_____

_____

What might they need from me to view me as REASONABLE/RATIONAL?

_____

_____

What might I need to do more/less of?

_____

_____

Personal feedback

_____

_____

WORKSHEET - Day 18

NAME OF PERSON _____ RELATIONSHIP_____

STATUS DIFFERENCE   (Circle one)   High to Low   Low to High   Equal

Interactional goal? _____

What might they need from me so they experience TRUST?

_____

_____

What might I need to do more/less of?

_____

_____

What might they need from me so they experience POSITIVE EMOTIONS?

_____

_____

What might I need to do more/less of?

_____

_____

What might they need from me to view me as REASONABLE/RATIONAL?

_____

_____

What might I need to do more/less of?

_____

_____

Personal feedback

_____

_____

WORKSHEET - Day 19

NAME OF PERSON _____ RELATIONSHIP_____

STATUS DIFFERENCE   (Circle one)   High to Low   Low to High   Equal

Interactional goal? _____

What might they need from me so they experience TRUST?

_____

_____

What might I need to do more/less of?

_____

_____

What might they need from me so they experience POSITIVE EMOTIONS?

_____

_____

What might I need to do more/less of?

_____

_____

What might they need from me to view me as REASONABLE/RATIONAL?

_____

_____

What might I need to do more/less of?

_____

_____

Personal feedback

_____

_____

30

NAME OF PERSON _____ RELATIONSHIP_____

STATUS DIFFERENCE   (Circle one)   High to Low   Low to High   Equal

Interactional goal? _____

What might they need from me so they experience TRUST?

_____

_____

What might I need to do more/less of?

_____

_____

What might they need from me so they experience POSITIVE EMOTIONS?

_____

_____

What might I need to do more/less of?

_____

_____

What might they need from me to view me as REASONABLE/RATIONAL?

_____

_____

What might I need to do more/less of?

_____

_____

Personal feedback

_____

_____

WORKSHEET - Day 21

NAME OF PERSON _____ RELATIONSHIP_____

STATUS DIFFERENCE   (Circle one)   High to Low   Low to High   Equal

Interactional goal? _____

What might they need from me so they experience TRUST?

_____

_____

What might I need to do more/less of?

_____

_____

What might they need from me so they experience POSITIVE EMOTIONS?

_____

_____

What might I need to do more/less of?

_____

_____

What might they need from me to view me as REASONABLE/RATIONAL?

_____

_____

What might I need to do more/less of?

_____

_____

Personal feedback

_____

_____

CONCLUSIONS for Days 15-21

Based upon your Shapiro 21 Day Approach findings, please answer the following:

1. What are 3 communication practices you can do *more* of?

_____

_____

_____

2. What reminders, tools or support would best allow you to do so?

_____

_____

_____

3. What are 3 communication practices you can do *less* of?

_____

_____

_____

4. What reminders, tools or support would best allow you to do so?

_____

_____

_____

WORKSHEET - Extra

NAME OF PERSON _____ RELATIONSHIP_____

STATUS DIFFERENCE   (Circle one)   High to Low   Low to High   Equal

Interactional goal? _____

What might they need from me so they experience TRUST?

_____

_____

What might I need to do more/less of?

_____

_____

What might they need from me so they experience POSITIVE EMOTIONS?

_____

_____

What might I need to do more/less of?

_____

_____

What might they need from me to view me as REASONABLE/RATIONAL?

_____

_____

What might I need to do more/less of?

_____

_____

Personal feedback

_____

_____

34

WORKSHEET - Extra

NAME OF PERSON _____ RELATIONSHIP_____

STATUS DIFFERENCE   (Circle one)   High to Low   Low to High   Equal

Interactional goal? _____

What might they need from me so they experience TRUST?

_____

_____

What might I need to do more/less of?

_____

_____

What might they need from me so they experience POSITIVE EMOTIONS?

_____

_____

What might I need to do more/less of?

_____

_____

What might they need from me to view me as REASONABLE/RATIONAL?

_____

_____

What might I need to do more/less of?

_____

_____

Personal feedback

_____

_____

WORKSHEET - Extra

NAME OF PERSON _____ RELATIONSHIP_____

STATUS DIFFERENCE   (Circle one)   High to Low   Low to High   Equal

Interactional goal? _____

What might they need from me so they experience TRUST?

_____

_____

What might I need to do more/less of?

_____

_____

What might they need from me so they experience POSITIVE EMOTIONS?

_____

_____

What might I need to do more/less of?

_____

_____

What might they need from me to view me as REASONABLE/RATIONAL?

_____

_____

What might I need to do more/less of?

_____

_____

Personal feedback

_____

_____

WORKSHEET - Extra

NAME OF PERSON _____ RELATIONSHIP_____

STATUS DIFFERENCE   (Circle one)   High to Low   Low to High   Equal

Interactional goal? _____

What might they need from me so they experience TRUST?

_____

_____

What might I need to do more/less of?

_____

_____

What might they need from me so they experience POSITIVE EMOTIONS?

_____

_____

What might I need to do more/less of?

_____

_____

What might they need from me to view me as REASONABLE/RATIONAL?

_____

_____

What might I need to do more/less of?

_____

_____

Personal feedback

_____

_____

NOTES

NOTES

NOTES

NOTES

HOW EFFECTIVE IS YOUR COMMUNICATION?

Based upon the Three Pillars of Exceptional Communication, the *Exceptionally Human®* *Communication Profile* is a simple online assessment tool that helps you recognize how other people might be experiencing your communication. In just a few minutes' time, you'll receive comprehensive feedback about your communication that you can immediately put to use on your journey towards becoming an *Exceptionally Human®* communicator!

www.shapirocommunications.com/profile

Shapiro

info@shapirocommunications.com
215.805.1695

Made in the USA
Middletown, DE
10 August 2020